Foods

by Jennifer Boothroyd

first step nonfiction

Lerner Publications Company · Minneapolis

We all eat food.

Spicy foods

Hot foods

Cold foods

Soft foods

Crunchy foods

What do you eat?